The Letters of John

Journeying Deeper Into the Johannine Epistles

ROGER DRUITT

Floris Books

Cover image: Roger Druitt

First published by Floris Books in 2022
© 2022 Roger Druitt
Roger Druitt has asserted his right under the
Copyright, Design and Patents Act 1988
to be identified as the Author of this Work

 Also available as an eBook

British Library CIP Data available
ISBN 978-178250-820-5
Printed in Great Britain by TJ Books

 Floris Books supports sustainable forest management by
printing this book on materials made from wood that
comes from responsible sources and reclaimed material

The Letters of John

Contents

Acknowledgments

Much appreciation to the many individuals and groups who studied this work with me over its 25 year incubation; and special thanks to David Bryer for his helpful critical reading at the later stages.

Introduction

The impulse to write this work arose through finding that the long-loved texts of the Letters of John are also elevated guidance for the health and development of Christian congregations. Gradually it became clear that the essence had such a quality as to be of substance not only for my 'home' church, The Christian Community, but for any congregation of Christianity. Most importantly, however, since the Letters are truly modern, in the sense of being totally without bias of race, colour, creed or any other classification, they can apply to any grouping of human souls. This quality of unbiased humanity has become the most treasured – and embattled – of modern life: to treat others as oneself, without definition. These Letters prompted me to make a translation that brings out these finer nuances.

As a child, the word 'abide', as in 'Abide with us…' worked its magic. Later, in my priest training, it was pointed out that this word, through Greek, was connected to 'man' and to 'manas'. In Rudolf Steiner's body of spiritual and mental research methods and results, called anthroposophy, he describes a scheme of human development through the centuries. This 'manas' is what we are developing now. 'Developing' rather than evolving, because humanity has reached the stage where positive evolution cannot be guaranteed: it requires hard striving, without which our evolution becomes a backsliding into less human conditions.

I traced 'abide' throughout the works of John. In his gospel there is to be found a characterisation of John (Chapter 21), that he will 'abide' until Christ's own revelation, in what is sometimes referred to as the Second Coming or *Parousia*. He has become a permanent presence albeit a hidden one.

The three Letters and three words

After *abide,* other words stood out, but also an idea: that the First Letter is a general 'handbook' for community life. The second, addressed to a lady, seemed to refer to the soul of this community – something which I found supported by tradition – while the third could be to a young priest whom John had prepared for his office.

These three Letters exemplify this in their different ways. The first is five chapters long. It is a thorough laying out of the central facts and feelings of Christianity and its main thrust is how these can *become real in a community.*

The Second Letter is addressed to a lady. From the content, one can, along with current thinking, easily discern that it is to the *congregation,* but as though to an individual. The hypothesis here is that this is the *soul* of the congregation, the unifying spiritual entity within the human diversity. There is a contrast here with the letters in the Apocalypse, addressed as they are to the angel of the congregation, to its *spirit.* But letters being physical things, they must be received by physical people, a saintly woman and a priest.

Although not itself an apocalyptic letter, the third is addressed to 'Gaius' and the contention is that this is a congregational priest, possibly newly ordained and maybe by John himself. The activity of the Antichrist that is so challenging in the Apocalypse is touched upon here too.

In the quest around *abide,* three other words appeared special for John's message, as he wrestled new possibilities from the language available to him. These are *righteousness, love* and *truth.* They are here shown to relate to the Trinity of Father, Son and Spirit. *Abide* is the way through which these qualities are mediated, both to Jesus the man through his incarnation and to us now, through the building of a community in the spirit of John. In John's Gospel, *abide* appears most frequently in Chapter 15 (verses 4–9), where the vine is used to illustrate community and where *abide* means the connecting relationship to Christ himself through (the life blood of) that community. It is also the pivotal word of the Letters, creating as it does a kind of overarching 'abode' in which the other three faculties can work on us as we attempt the challenge of modern communal life. The sections on each of these words in Chapter 5 unfold this. This figure is like that of the human being with the three soul faculties of thinking, feeling and will, which we have to bring into harmony through the power of our 'I'. When our 'I' links livingly to the great cosmic 'I', like the branch to the vine, then this harmonious soul links in *love* to the Trinity, where it finds its brother and sister *righteousness* and *truth.*

Translation of the
Letters of John

Note

Some verses are paraphrased and expanded to bring out the meaning, prompted during the flow of the translation work. These are shown in [square brackets] in the text, and are meant as an aid to understanding, and on no account as a correction.

The 'special' words to help grasp texts such as *righteousness, love, truth, abide, sin* and *commandment* are indicated in the margins by R, L, T, A, S, and C.

The Greek word for 'sin' derives from missing the mark, the aim, or falling short, rather than the modern etymology of being divided (sin, asunder). This is brought out regarding the devil (1Jn 3:8) and in the context of mortal sin (1Jn 5:16). The sin of the Antichrist, however, is not in *missing* his aim. His aim is itself *anti*-Christ: he will only be made to miss it through the good powers described in these Letters – through the efforts of living human communities that have made these aims their own. We shall see that John's conception of sin (actually Christ's), and the resolving of it, is very different from that in many of our modern minds, whether we feel under a yoke of guilt or find ourselves in rebellion against accepting any meaning for 'sin' at all. It is actually quite a good beginning to a modern spiritual life to take on building one's own conception of sin and not using those of others.

The First Letter of John

He that was of the beginning
Whom we have heard
Whom we have seen with our eyes
Whom we have looked upon and touched
with our hands
THE WORD OF LIFE –
² and that Life was clearly revealed;
and we have seen and do bear witness;
and declare to you:
life eternal, which was with the Father
and was clearly revealed to us.

³ He whom we have seen and heard we now declare also to you, that you may walk together with us in the forecourt of communion, which is indeed our fellowship with the Father and with his Son Jesus Christ. ⁴ We are writing these things to you that our joy be full. ⁵ This then is the spirit tiding we have heard from him and proclaim to you, namely, that God is light and there is no darkness present in him at all. ⁶ If we then say we have fellowship with him and yet are walking in the dark, we speak a lie and are
T not practising truth. ⁷ But if we are walking in

6 Jn 11:10

the light, as he has his being in the light, we are in communion with one another and the blood of Jesus his Son cleanses us from all sin.   S

⁸ If we say that we are without sin we are S deceiving ourselves and that spirit essence called truth [which should flow out through his blood, T through our fellowship, creating an earthly home for Father and Son to dwell in spirit with us] is not in us.

⁹ If we confess our sin [and so grasp it with S our destiny] he pours his healing power into our heart as faith and conveys to our bodies the upright light-body of his Father. He will unite his redeeming life with our destiny and cleanse R us from the crookedness and dross which hinder the invasion of this light.

¹⁰ If we deny being subject to the sickness of sin, we make his existing a lie and his word is not in us.

2

My little children, I write you these things so that you do not miss your spiritual aim and S thereby sin. But if anyone does sin we have in S Jesus Christ a guide and comforter to lead us back on to the path to the Father, since he bears the Father's straight body of light. ² For it is he R who through his sacrifice reintegrates our sins S into his own redeeming life – and not ours only but also those of the whole world.

³ This is how we know that we have known him: that we keep to the aim he sets before C

---

8 Jn 15:7–9; Jn 14:10–17   2:1 1Jn 1:3,7; Jn 15:26

our spirit. ⁴Whoever says, I know him, without
C T cherishing his aims, is a liar: in this person truth
has no place. ⁵But whoever keeps his word,
T L truly God's love has been made perfect in him.
Through this we know that we have our being
A in him. ⁶Whoever says he dwells in him will also
want to walk in the way that he walked.

L ⁷Beloved, I am not writing you a new objec-
C C tive but the original spirit objective, which you
C had from the very outset. This original aim is to
receive the Logos, the Word which you heard
[– the creative Word of life and light]. ⁸Yet at
C the same time I *am* writing you a new objective,
for what was true in him is now also true in
T you, because the darkness is past and true light is
already shining. ⁹Whoever says he is in the light
but hates his brother is still in darkness; ¹⁰but
L whoever loves his brother, [to the point of offer-
A ing his own destiny to serve the other's,] creates
for himself a new soul garment of spirit light [–
in which empathy can dissolve away any imped-
iment to the relationship]. ¹¹But whoever hates
his brother is in the darkness and is walking in
the darkness still; he does not know where he is
going because the darkness has blinded his eyes.

¹²I am writing to you, little children, because
S through his Name your missed aims have been
re-adjusted, and their consequences will be car-
ried into future destiny. ¹³I am writing to you,
fathers, because you have come to know him
who has begun a new generation. I am writing

11 Jn 11:10

to you, young men, because you have vanquished the evil one. [14] I wrote to you, young children, because you have come to know the Father. I wrote to you, fathers, because you have come to know him who is the Beginning. I wrote to you, young men, because you are in full vigour and the Logos of God dwells in you, [his Word A weaving within you a new garment of humanity,] and you have vanquished the evil one.

[15] Do not make your love-sacrifice to the L world or the things of the world. If anyone loves L the world, the love-sacrifice to the Father can- L not come to life in him [16] because all that is in the visible world,

the lust of the flesh [that fetters our body],
the lust of the eyes [that fetters our soul],
the vainglory of life [that diverts us from our
   path of destiny].

is not of the Father but of the world of work already wrought.

[17] For this wrought world is passing away and along with it the earthly desire for it; but he who is working the will of God makes an abiding A place of communion for future times.

[18] Young children, it is the final hour, and as you have heard, Antichrist is coming; even now many such antichrists have arisen, from which you can tell that a final hour has come. [19] They went forth from us but were not of us, for if they had been of us they would have remained in abiding communion with us, but it had to A

17 1Jn 2:19, 24   19 1Jn 2:17, 24

come to light that they were not all of us. [20] But, through the Holy One, you bear an anointing through which you can have insight into all that is living in the community.

[21] I have written to you not because you do
T not know the truth but because you *do* know
T it, and because no lie is of the truth. [Thus the angel of the community, who is inspired by the Spirit of Truth, draws together those who are the true souls of the congregation and separates off those who are only apparently so.] [22] Who is an untrue member if not he who denies that Jesus is the Christ? This is the opponent of Christ, who negates not only the Father but the Son also. [23] Whoever denies the Son loses the Father as well; whoever confesses the Son gains the Father too [– because the Son leads to him].

[24] Let what you heard from the spirit of new
A beginning prepare in you an abiding place for future communion. If what you heard from the
A beginning does become such an abode in you,
A you will abide there in communion with both the Son and the Father. [25] And this is the Spirit-word he promised us: life beyond cycles of time.

[26] I have written these things about those who will lead you astray. [27] But the anointing you received from him has established in you
A an abiding presence and you have no need for anyone to teach you about it. His anointing itself teaches you about everything: it unites
T you to the true spirit of the community and

is no lie. Abide in that spirit as he taught you. A
²⁸ And now little children, abide in this spirit of A
the community, which, through your anointing,
is a part of the being of the Son, so that when
he is revealed we may proclaim it confidently
and have no shame before him in his presence.
²⁹ If you realise that he bears in himself God's
straight light of being, realise also that whoever R
works out of this light in his own being has R
been born out of him.

3

Look at the nature of the love the Father has L
bestowed upon us for us to be called, and indeed
be, children of God, growing under his guidance. This is why the world cannot understand
our mystery: it does not know him.

² Beloved, we are now children of God but it L
has not yet been shown what we shall become;
yet we know that we shall become like him for
we shall see him with our sight as he really is.
³ Everyone nurturing this hope in him purifies
himself through the pure being that *he* is.

⁴ Everyone missing this aim in his deeds will s
also lack any other direction in life; and this sin s
brings lawlessness. ⁵ You know that the Son was
sent to shine forth upon the world to carry our
sins: there is no sin in him [– he does not fail to s s
reach his aim]. ⁶ No-one who builds their soul- A
life for the future through him misses their aim; s
but sinners do neither see nor know him. s

⁷ Little children, let no-one deceive you.

---

2 Jn 1: 18   3 Jn 15: 2–3   7 1Jn 2: 1

R Whoever brings the straight light of God's
R goodness into his actions is himself an upright
light-bearer after the light-bearing nature of the
S Christ. [8] Whoever sins by confusing his aims is of
the devil [– the world-confuser –] who already
S missed his aim in his high spiritual rank. The
Son of God was shown forth for this reason:
to unravel the devil's tangling work. [9] Whoever
S is begotten of God does not miss his aim in
A his doings, because his seed abides in him and
S he cannot sin because he is conceived of God.
[10] Thereby is it revealed who are the children
of God and who are the children of the devil.
R Whoever does not bring the straight light of
God into his deeds and the warmth of self-
L sacrifice in love towards his brother: he is not
of God. [11] For this is the spirit word which you
L heard from the beginning, that we should love
each other, not as Cain who was infected by the
evil one and slew his brother. [12] And why did
he slay him? Because his work was evil; but his
R brother's bore God's good light.
[13] Brothers and sisters, do not be surprised
if the world hates you. [14] We know that we
have crossed the threshold from death into life
L because we love [– and so share our destiny
with –] the other members of the congrega-
L A tion. Those not finding this kind of love remain
clad in the mantle of death. [15] Everyone hating
his brother extinguishes his humanity and you
know that this type of murderer is not wearing

a mantle of life lasting beyond time. ¹⁶Through A
this we know the nature of love, that he spread L
his living soul over us; and we ought to extend
our living souls for other members of the congregation in the same way.

¹⁷ Whoever has the world's goods, yet sees his
fellow man in need and closes his will against
him, how can God's love make itself at home in L A
him?

¹⁸ Little children, let us not love in word or in L
speech but in deeds and within the living truth T
of the congregation. ¹⁹ In this way we shall know
ourselves to be part of the living spirit of true T
community and before him our heart will stand
firm. ²⁰ But even when our heart cannot grasp
where we stand and our conscience troubles us,
we know that God is greater than our heart and
knows the full circumstances of our deeds.

²¹ Beloved, when our heart does not con-
demn us we may have confidence in God
²² and we may receive from him whatever we
ask because we keep his spiritual goal in our C
sight. Then we do what is pleasing to his sight.
²³ And this is his spirit aim: that we should open C
a heart-relationship with the Name of his Son
Jesus Christ and love one another according to L
the aim he gave us in spirit. ²⁴ He who keeps this C
aim abides in him; and he in him. Through this C A
we know that he is building a new soul in us, A
out of the spirit he has given to us.

4

L Beloved, do not put your faith in every spirit, but test the spirits, whether they be of God, because many false prophets have gone out into the world. ²You can tell the spirit of God by this: every spirit that acknowledges Jesus Christ having come in the flesh is of God ³ and every spirit that does not confess Jesus in this way is not of God; and this is of the Antichrist, which you have heard is coming, and is in the world even now.

⁴You are of God, little children, and have been victorious over all these things because he who is in you is greater than he who is in the world. ⁵The others are of the world and therefore their inspired words are of the world and the world listens to them. ⁶We are of God: those who also know God hear us but those not of God do not hear us. We can tell by this those of the spirit of
T truth from those of the spirit of error.

L L ⁷ Beloved, let us love each other because
L L love is of God and all who love are born of God
L and know God. ⁸ He who is not loving does not
L know God because God has his being in love.
L ⁹ God's love was shown forth in us in this, that God sent his once-born Son into the world so that we could live through him.

L L ¹⁰ Love consists in this, not that we loved God
L but that he loved us and sent his Son, so that
S through his sacrifice our sins could be woven
L into his redeeming life. ¹¹ Beloved, if God has
L L loved us in this way we ought also to love one another. ¹² No-one has ever beheld God. If we

love one another, God makes his dwelling in L A
us, [unfolding the members of his being in our
being,] and his love is brought to perfection in L
us.

[13] Through this we know that our future
soul-life is woven in him and his in us: he has A
given us of his spirit-breath [14] and we have seen
and do bear witness that the Father has sent the
Son as saviour of the world. [15] Whoever confesses that Jesus is the Son of God, God weaves A
his soul into him and his in God. [16] We also have
received God's love into the ways of our minds L
and hearts. God is love and whoever builds his L A
future soul-life through love abides in God and L A
God abides in him.   A

[17] For this, love has been brought to perfec- L
tion in us, that in the day of the parting of the
ways we may have confidence that we stand in
the world just as he does. [18] There is no fear in
love, but love casts out fear as it is perfected. Fear L L
has torment; and whoever fears has not been
perfected in love. [19] We are loving because he L L
first loved us. [20] If anyone says, I love God, yet L L
hates brother or sister, he is a liar, for whoever
does not love the brother or sister that he has L
seen cannot love the God that he has not seen. L

[21] And this is the spiritual task we have from C
him: that whoever loves God should also love L L
brother and sister.

14 Jn 20   16 1Jn 2:17, 19, 24

5

Everyone who believes that Jesus is the Christ, the Messiah, is begotten of God and everyone
L L loving the begetter also loves the begotten.

L   ²We know that we love the children of
L God whenever we love God himself and work
C towards his task for us in spirit. ³ For this is God's
L C love: that we keep to his spiritual tasks; and these
C tasks are not burdensome ⁴ because everything born of God vanquishes the world; and this is the victory that vanquishes the world — [the power that develops in our heart when we are relating to Jesus Christ,] our power of faith. ⁵ And who can vanquish the world if not he who believes that Jesus is the Son of God?

⁶ This is he who enters by water and by blood, Jesus Christ; not in water alone but in water and blood; and the breath of the Spirit is
T the witness because the Spirit is the truth. ⁷ For there are three that bear witness in the heavens: the Father, the Word and the Holy Spirit and the three are in the one; ⁸ and there are three that bear witness on earth: the wind, the water and the blood, and these three are in the one.

⁹ We may receive the testimony of men, yet the witness of God is greater, for this is the witness of God: he has testified to his Son. ¹⁰ Whoever relates to the Son in his heart has this witness within himself. Whoever does not believe in God has made him a liar because he has not taken into his heart the testimony that

3 Jn 15   9 Jn 5:31f; Jn 20:31

God has testified about his Son. [11] And this is the testimony: God gave life to us for all cycles of time and this life is in his Son.

[12] He who has the Son has life, he who has not God's Son has not life.

[13] I have written these things to you who, believing, have taken the Name of the Son of God into your hearts, that you may know that you now do have that eternal life that is intended for those who do believe in the Son of God. [14] And this is the confidence we have with him, that if we ask anything that is within his will, he hears us, [15] and if we know that he hears us whatever we ask, we know that we have had a response to those things we ask of him even though we are not aware of it.

[16] If anyone sees his brother committing a sin that is not a mortal sin, he shall intercede s for him and he will give him life through the power of prayer, where the sin is not leading to s a death of soul. There is sin which leads to death s of soul but I am not referring to that when I say to intercede.* [17] Everything done outside the good straight light of God has missed the aim R S and there is this type of sin which is not mor- s tal. [18] We know that everyone begotten of God does not sin in this way for the One begotten s of God keeps him and the evil one does not touch him.

13 Jn 20:31; 1Jn 3:23   14 Jn 16:24
15 Mt 6:8   16 Ac 5:1–11
* A sin committed against the community is against the Holy Spirit, hence a mortal sin.

[19] We know that we are of God and that the whole world lies in the hands of the evil one. [20] On the other hand we know that the Son of God has come and has given us a penetrating mind that we might discover the real being of T T truth. And we are one with the being of truth T in his Son Jesus Christ. This is God the true one and the life that transcends time.

[21] Little children, guard yourselves from the images of gods which lack this life. Amen.

The Second Letter of John

The elder to the chosen lady of wisdom,* [who
overshines the congregation as the soul of
the community] and to those who are grow-
L ing spiritually within her, whom I love in the
truth [I share my spirit with them and would
extend my life towards them as part of the true
spirit-life of the community]. Yet I do this not
as an individual but together with all who have
TT known this Spirit of Truth; ² through the truth
A that abides in us, [weaving its soul-dwelling
around and between us,] completing with us the
task of the age.

³ Grace, mercy and peace are to be with
us through God the Father and through Jesus
Christ the Son of the Father in the light of this
TL truth and the warmth of this love.

⁴ I rejoiced greatly when I found those
growing in your care walking in this Spirit of
TC Truth according to the aims we received from
the Father. ⁵ And now I pray you, lady, not by
C writing you a new aim but one we had from
the spirit of a new beginning, namely that we
L should cause love to grow between us. ⁶ This is
LC love, that we should walk with the aim he has

* An honorary form of address to a congregation.
5 1Jn 2:24

31

put before us. This is his aim, as you heard from C
the beginning that we should walk with it.

⁷ For many deceivers went out into the world,
ones not confessing Jesus Christ coming in the
flesh; this is the deceiver and the Antichrist.

⁸ Look to yourselves, lest you lose what we
have achieved: rather receive its full benefit.

⁹ Anyone who goes forth without remain- A
ing part of the community woven in Christ's
teaching no longer has God: whoever abides A
by his word, letting it bring order to his soul,
has both the Father and the Son [– the Father
through the shared aim of selfless love and the
Son through its realisation]. ¹⁰ If anyone comes
to you without wearing the garment woven of
this teaching, do not receive him into the house-
hold and do not speak to him the greeting of joy.
¹¹ Whoever does give him the greeting of joy is
uniting themselves with his evil deeds.

¹² Although I have much to write to you I
intend not to use paper and ink but hope rather
to come to you, growing towards you, and speak
in inspiration, mouth to mouth, to bring our joy
to fulfilment.

¹³ Those growing within the soul of your chosen sister community send you their greetings.

12 Rv 1:3

The Third Letter of John

L L The elder to Gaius the beloved, whom I love
T in the truth [with whom I share my spirit and
for whom I would extend my life, within the
L true spirit of the community]. ² Beloved, I pray
that you prosper in everything and are of good
health, as you feel in your soul to be on the right
path.

³ I was delighted when some members came
and told in witness of your relationship to the
T true soul of the congregation just as you, in your
T spirit, walk in the Spirit of Truth. ⁴ I have no
greater joy than this, than to hear that my pupils
T walk freely within the true soul of the com-
L munity. ⁵ Beloved, whatever you do, whether
for members or strangers, you do it in heart's
L faith. ⁶ They bore witness of the fire of your love
before the church. You shall do well by helping
them progress in a right attitude of worthiness
towards God, ⁷ for they went forth purely in the
Name, not relying on the inborn talents of their
own nature. ⁸ We should therefore support such
people that they become co-workers with us in
T the Spirit of Truth.

⁹ I wrote something to the congregation but
that Diotrephes who likes to be superior would
not acknowledge us; ¹⁰ so if I come I will remind

him of his doings: he prates with evil words against us; and, not being satisfied with that, neither receives our members nor permits those to join who would, but bars them and throws them out of the congregation.

[11] Beloved, do not copy the bad but imitate L the good. The doer of the good is God; the doer of the bad has not seen God.

[12] Demetrius has received testimony from everybody, not least from the truth living in the T congregation as a whole. We also testify to him and you know that our testimony has come through the Spirit of Truth. T

[13] I had much to write to you but do not wish to write with ink and pen as [14] I hope to see you very soon and we will speak inspired words mouth to mouth.

[15] Peace be with you. Our friends send you their greetings. Greet the friends there in the Name.

Commentary

1

Orientation

Background

The Christian community of the first century was a place where soul care was administered and the first services held, possibly in a less definite form than now. When they had grown beyond what could be served directly by the twelve Apostles, the office of deacon was instituted to cover needs during and between priestly visits (Acts 6). Men were chosen through their social, pastoral and spiritual qualities. Stephen, the first martyr, was one of them. Acts well portrays the vibrancy and trials of this time and the new reader may well be amazed at the excitement and pace of the story. The background and community life were held together as a living organism by the committed women, who are occasionally mentioned.

On the other hand there were those whose personal ambitions hindered them from seeing what these new communities meant, using them merely as an opportunity for their own self-esteem and standing. The First Letter refers to 'untrue members' of the community, even aligning them to 'Antichrist'. The third mentions

Diotrephes in this connection of personal agenda. It was into this new and volatile situation that the Presbyter (Elder), John, wrote his Letters or Epistles.

John

Who was John? There have been various ideas, connected to those named John in the New Testament, and it is unclear whether the different names refer to the same man. There is *John the Apostle,* the disciple of Jesus, son of Zebedee, brother of James, who may be the same as *John the Evangelist,* the author of the Gospel of John and – as many scholars believe – the three Letters. Research still seeks whether this is so. Then comes *John of Patmos* (sometimes called John the Divine), the author of the Book of Revelation, whose identity is likewise under research. For the reasons that follow, the present work ascribes the three texts to a single author.

'Simon, son of John, do you love me?' asks Jesus of Peter by the lakeside, some time after the Resurrection (Jn 21). Peter was called Simon bar Jona, that is, son of Jona/Jonah/Iona; but *son of Jona* is also a title used in the mysteries, referring back to the Old Testament prophet Jonah, renowned for his adventure in the storm and his three nights of initiation in the belly of the great fish, a state of soul in the deepest recesses of the body, reaching out to the Lord in the heights for succour. Referred to here (and expanded by the wonderful hymn to God recorded in the Book of Job) is the pre-Christian foreshadowing of Christ's three days in the grave, the final preparation for Resurrection. The Raphael cartoon in the Victoria and Albert Museum of this scene shows Peter standing still, while another figure is already hastening towards Jesus, the only movement in the whole picture; and this other figure, as we may deduce from John's narrative, is the 'beloved disciple', a phrase that connects to the quotation at the beginning of this paragraph, and the one who is already 'following', whilst Peter is still asking questions.

We here take that line of theological research of the early twentieth century that identifies him with Lazarus, who took the title John, or Ioannes, from the time of his raising. Independently, Steiner made the same conclusion but added that, in addition to the risen Lazarus 'qualifying' for the title of John through his initiation, he was influenced in a special way by the spirit of John the Baptist, who had by then been beheaded. 'Lazarus-John' is the first of those initiated by Christ himself; first in his own raising, then also through his experiences following Christ's own encounter with and transforming of death. The gospel makes it clear, in subtle ways to preserve the mystery, that this Lazarus-John is the writer of the Gospel of John, rather than John the son of Zebedee, the more widespread idea.

The opening lines of the First Letter so resemble parts of the prologue to the Gospel of John, that to suggest a John other than the Evangelist to write with such intimacy would be unfruitful. Likewise, the Apocalypse, when read thoroughly, manifests the same spirit.

Lazarus-John is so named first because he was initiated in the Iona stream and secondly, because the angelic spirit of John the Baptist overshone him.

For Steiner, the above picture of John as Lazarus came in a way similar to his other research, but he gave the following connections as aids to taking it in. Lazarus-John's being had gone through several stages before the raising of Lazarus. In his life, which included special pupilship of Jesus, he had fulfilled the stages of initiation in the ancient mysteries, except the final calling forth. This he could not do through his own merit and so he was in a state equivalent to death. Jesus, his teacher, had to perform the final act, that of the raising. Steiner also points to the profundity of the opening of John's Gospel as an indication that what lies therein is of a mystery nature not elsewhere described, and not just a narrative. By noting John's background in the mysteries, his unique descriptions of the raising of Lazarus, the transformation in Lazarus' being afterwards, and the phrase 'beloved disciple' for both Lazarus and the Evangelist, he makes this piece of research more accessible. These are not proofs but pointers.*

John the beloved disciple

In wondering whether we can accept this piece of spiritual research – that Evangelist, beloved disciple and Lazarus are one and the same – we may weigh the following. It was the 'beloved disciple' of Jesus Christ who leaned on his breast after the supper while he spoke his departing words to the others. These chapters of the Gospel of John (13–17) contain some of the most intimate details and images ever written and thus suggest an influence beyond that of ordinary life. As Lazarus he had been personally raised from death, unlike Jonah, who was brought forth again by the elements under the direction of Yahweh. Jesus' act in public precipitated his final persecution by the religious authorities.

Later, Lazarus–John alone had stood with Jesus' mother beneath the cross (the gospel notes that all the other disciples had fled) and witnessed the flow of blood from the lance wound. Note the emphatic way he expresses this testimony: 'One of the soldiers pierced his side with a lance, and at once blood and water flowed. He who saw

---

* See Steiner, *Christianity as Mystical Fact*, and lectures 7 and 8 of *The Gospel of John*.

it has borne witness, and his testimony is true. He knows that he is telling the truth, so that you also may see it with your heart.' (Jn 19:34f) The First Letter also refers to it (1Jn 5).

Steiner has pointed out something that we too can experience in our lives. Whether as parent and child, pupil and teacher or perhaps manager and team member, when a certain relationship is established of trust, respect, willingness and openness, we can sense a new kind of feeling that transcends the more usual ones. Something of a preparedness to serve the other arises. This relationship is referred to by Steiner as one that used to belong only in the mysteries, but which in our age can be found or created right across life. John in the Gospel calls it 'beloved' and the love that underpins it is meant in a higher sense than the more usual meanings of the word. Its usage is probably a more telling link of authorship of Gospel, Letters and Apocalypse than other valuable research.

Another connection, alluded to above, is that between John the Baptist and Lazarus. Amazingly, in his *Isenheim Altarpiece,* the artist Matthias Grünewald has depicted them both standing under the cross. The illustration is like a composite supersensible reality, for the Baptist was of course dead long before the crucifixion. But observing the composition of John's Gospel we find that the Baptist features in Chapter 1 and at the end of Chapter 10; Chapter 11 tells of the raising of Lazarus (introduced there for the first time); while the remaining ten chapters describe the events of Palm Sunday on into the Resurrection. The composition shows a Baptist half and a Lazarus/beloved disciple half, linked by the raising of Lazarus–John. In an artistic work of this kind, such a composition is a significant message.

We therefore will take Lazarus as the author of the Gospel, the three Letters and the Book of Revelation or Apocalypse. This is not a theological proof but an experiential hint, developed in what follows.

John and the Apocalypse

During his exile on Patmos, John had the vision of Christ's revelations as Son of Man, recorded as the Book of Revelation. Later still he wrote his Gospel, to make available to humanity the Resurrection through a book of word-pictures. The Letters bring the spiritual fruits of his initiation and experience of Christ into his congregations.

Apocalypse is a significant word when compared to its partner, Epiphany. *Epiphany* is Christ's appearance upon the world stage at the Baptism (Jn 1). The word means a 'shining out upon' (the world). *Apocalypse* on the other hand means an uncovering, a drawing back of the veil. We meet it in Novalis' work, *The Disciple of Sais,* where the youth draws back the veil of the goddess Isis and falls dead through the overpowering force of the experience. The Apocalypse draws back the veil of death to reveal Christ as spirit being in contrast with the incarnated man of the ministry. It is a powerful book, 'bitter in the belly' (Rv 10:9). The Letters grow out of this followed finally by the Gospel, a work so sculpted and ordered as to enable the reader to discover the reality of its truths by experiencing the flow of the images.

We shall go more deeply into the fruits of Lazarus–John's experience at the Last Supper in the essays that follow. This is indeed the main purpose of the present work: to re-enliven biblical expressions that to some ears have become rather hackneyed, and to bring new spirit and strength to the wide variety of the Christian communities of today. The Greek text has been rendered to this end, utilising the anthroposophical view of the make-up of modern human beings and their evolution. Here, John's work plays an important part. It is hoped that it finds its place in the freer attitudes of modern times.

2

Detail

The work of redemption: love and the Holy Trinity

John distinguished within the Godhead the three holy members of the Trinity through the way he had come to know Jesus. Their pupil-teacher relationship, described in the Introduction, is expressed in the language of the mysteries as *love*. It is a relationship where there is mutual giving and receiving: both pupil and teacher gain, progressing upon their respective paths. The Gospel (Chapter 11) states clearly that Jesus *loved* John and his two sisters, Mary and Martha. This is said of no-one else and indicates their unique bond. For John, it meant reaching the death process which was to transform him into the first Christian initiate; for Jesus it was an essential step towards his own resurrection. As we noted, Lazarus is called John as a kind of title, one who has gone through a death trial, like Jonah, who gave his name to the process with its three vowels *I, O* and *A*. The vowel *I* (sounding as *ee*) reveals an uprightness, the *O* (long *oh*) a sense of wonder and embracing, and *A* (also long) that other sense of wonder that opens out to the world and the future.

So, within the Trinity, John saw first the Son, who in Jesus had become the brother of humanity ('he knew what was in man,' Jn 2:25); secondly, the Father who had sent him (Jn 13:20) and who would, at his death, soon receive him again; and finally the Spirit whom the Son promised to send (Jn 16:7: 'if I go I shall send him to you'). This Trinity appears in more detail in 1Jn 5:6-8:

This is he who enters by water and by blood,
Jesus Christ; not in water alone but in water and
blood; and the breath of the Spirit is the witness
because the Spirit is the truth. For there are three
that bear witness in the heavens: the Father, the
Word and the Holy Spirit and the three are in
the one; and there are three that bear witness on
earth: the wind, the water and the blood, and
these three are in the one.

How such a text may be understood is significant to the whole of John's conception of the relationship of the Holy Trinity to earthly substances and hence to those of the Eucharist: bread, water and wine. For John, the Trinity is the mode of working into humanity of a God who is after all, and before all, One. His powerful witnessing of the flow of blood *and* water from the cross connects this wonderful verse with the practice of using wine *and* water in the sacrament.

But what relevance has all this today, when we are differently constituted in mind and soul and are generally without the mantle of faith and religious practice around us that was part of life a few generations ago? Is there something deeply buried in John's Letters that can germinate most fruitfully in just such a soil as is the soul of a modern person with their positive scepticism, independent individuality and spiritual quest?

The four parts of the human being and their healing

Steiner's image of the human being is needed for a good grasp of what is presented here and is instrumental in discovering how the forces of righteousness, love and truth help develop new elements within us, both in individuals and in the community. Steiner accepted current conceptions but mainly as they apply to the *material* being that we are. But instead of ascribing the fact that we are *alive* to functions of this physical apparatus, he attributes it to a subtle body, a distinct and non-physical entity, which he calls the ethereal or ether body (nothing to do with the nineteenth century concept of ether). He also points out *where* in the physical body the effects of this ethereal body can be observed: life processes such as growth, digestion, self-healing, reproduction and the influence of the glandular system upon the whole body.

A further step is to observe that all these processes are affected by something likewise beyond them, such as mood. All the life processes, and hence our health, are affected by mood. None of this is new in Steiner except his ascribing it to an 'astral body', so called for its affinity to the planetary world surrounding and embracing the earth, just as the ethereal or etheric body is linked in to the elements of earth, water, air and fire as described by the science of the Middle Ages. This astral body is related to what can also be termed soul, and brings about our inner activities of thought, action and feeling.

Yet every time you pass over the box of chocolates, you are aware that there is also an inner force with which you can override what are sometimes very powerful urges. Steiner calls this the ego or I. (One has to keep the meaning independent of other modern usage of psychology until one has grasped the wider concepts within his works, when all becomes more straightforward.)

In this way we have the four members of the human being. This is but the barest outline. Steiner's book *Theosophy* contains the basic teaching on the subject. Other works go further into the mutual reactions between the members, for example our state of vitality affects our mood just as the reverse is true. However, once we have started these observations we will never again be able to see ourselves as merely a piece of matter with electrochemical impulses. Instead we will identify with our basic 'impulse' as working out of the 'I', the entelechy, potentially free in so far as it attains a free relationship with the determinative influences of the lower three members. It becomes a true aim to transform these by working out of our highest.

It is this transforming that is pivotal to our whole life on earth because once something is achieved it can be kept forever if we are careful. Most of us experience the necessity of repeatedly giving up a habit we want to drop. It works for a while, then we slide; but this just demonstrates the self-perpetuating power that exists within the ethereal body (where habits reside) in contrast to the more 'airy' quality of the astral body. The latter will give up and let its wind blow elsewhere unless we are determined to persevere and bring our true spirit into play. Here it is seen within our language how 'I' is a spiritual entity, belonging to a realm beyond the influence of the 'astral' world. 'I' have the power to transform 'me', my soul, even 'my-self'!

The fourfold human being and the four stages of the ministry

In the three years of Christ's ministry there are four stages. At each stage the four parts of the human being outlined above are successively transformed.

The four processes that illustrate the raising and healing of the four human principles appear in the Gospel as
follows:

- In the *Temptation* it is the 'I' itself that wins free. Jesus,
  in his inner being, is not drawn into a misuse of his
  divine powers for earthly ends.
- In the *Feeding of the Five Thousand* we see the soul of
  Jesus become bountiful under the influence of the
  starry world through which the sun passes in the
  course of the year (represented by the twelve baskets).
  This apparently unfounded assertion may be reached
  through the mood of the Gospel narrative married
  to the image of such a location (Jn 6). Christ and
  the twelve disciples mirror this cosmic configuration,
  bringing those powers down on to the earth.
- At the *Transfiguration,* Jesus' face and body become
  radiant like sun, showing the vital, or ethereal, body
  shining with life instead of being dark with mortality.
  The sun in the sky is the outer marker of the etheric
  sphere of life that draws earthly life towards it, as seen in
  the upward growth of plants; now this state is brought
  to life within the constitution of Jesus. He is the life,
  and the light, as the prologue in John's Gospel notes.
- Finally, in *Holy Week,* beginning with the ride on the
  ass and foal (Mt 21:5, 7), and especially from the Last
  Supper to the resurrection, it is the physical body itself
  that is transformed. This is prophesied in Jesus' words on
  Palm Sunday (Jn 12:24) about the seed grain needing
  to die in the earth before it can multiply. This 'fore-
  shines' the multiplying of resurrection substance in Holy
  Communion, to act thereafter as a leaven of resurrection
  within our own constitution – a medicine against the
  death of the soul and ultimately the body too, a mystery
  that goes beyond what we can portray here.

Anthroposophy has indicated that this successive transformation also enables aspects of Jesus Christ's resurrected fourfold constitution to be incorporated into us human beings, thereby gradually enhancing all of human life.

For a complete healing of the human makeup, it had first to be freed from mortality before being imbued with the work of the divine Spirit. The resurrection achieved this, and part of that healing is still continuing. Contemplating these events, we can glimpse the complexity of the deed of Christ the Redeemer.

The transformation of the fourfold human being

In his description in *Theosophy*, Steiner leads from a fourfold to a sevenfold human being, where as a result of perfecting the transformation of the *astral body* by our striving spirit (and it takes a great deal of striving to achieve anything lasting) a new aspect of human nature becomes part of us. This he calls *Spirit Self* (or *manas*). Furthermore, the transformed *ethereal body* engenders *Life Spirit (buddhi)* and finally the transformed *physical body* becomes *Spirit Man (atman)*. This is a glimpse into a far future.

The main thesis of this work is to illustrate John's Letters as an aid in this process through the life of a Christian congregation. We shall focus particularly on Spirit Self. The earlier, eastern term for this was *manas*, a Sanskrit word that appears frequently in the Greek of the Letters as *menein*, usually rendered as 'abide'. This word is picked out here as the most relevant for our time.

Remembering the triad of *righteousness, love* and *truth*, and its connection to the Holy Trinity, we may consider the following. When John calls Christ the 'mediator and advocate' (1Jn 2:1), an expression used in the Anglican Eucharist, he is pointing to Christ as the one who helps the human 'I' or ego in this attaining of Spirit Self, Life Spirit and Spirit Man. In regarding the fourfold makeup of the human being, we can now note that the 'I' has a dual nature. It is the pinnacle of the natural being and the seed of the spiritual one. It is our innermost part yet the place where our future spirit is to unfold. Spirit Self, Life Spirit and Spirit Man are, with this aspect of the 'I', a fourfold spiritual being in spiritual space.

To reach this goal, it is just those qualities succinctly touched upon in the third verse of the Second Letter – grace, mercy and peace – that our 'I' needs to aid this triple transformation. John writes as though he expects his listener to understand him, but as we might not be in such a privileged position they are treated in their own right in the essays.

When these three gifts of blessing 'abide' with us, are given a lodging or dwelling place within us, and remain there, they begin weaving these higher members into our being. The body of Christ, the lifeblood of Christ and the soul-peace of Christ will then 'be with us through God the Father and through Jesus Christ the Son of the Father in the light of this truth and the warmth of this love' (2Jn 3).

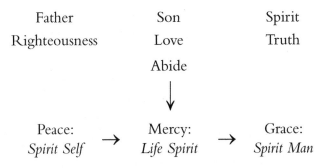

Father   Son   Spirit

Righteousness   Love   Truth

Abide

Peace: Mercy: Grace:
Spirit Self → *Life Spirit* → *Spirit Man*

The next two chapters try to demonstrate this, starting with what John actually wrote, and then drawing pictures and deductions from that, rather than bringing concepts and ideas from outside.

3

Fellowship: the Union of God and Humanity

A key word in many streams of modern Christianity, but one that is possibly off-putting for some as a phrase that might feel superficial, is 'fellowship'. It is a word worth considering afresh to see whether it can be deepened. We shall look at the passages that contain it or related expressions, such as 'being born of', 'communion with' and so on, and compose our understanding from what John actually says.

Going to the last verses, we read,

> We know that we are of God and that the whole world lies in the hands of the evil one. On the other hand we know that the Son of God has come and has given us a penetrating mind that we might discover the real being of truth. And we are one with the being of truth in his Son Jesus Christ. This is God the true one and the life that transcends time.
>
> Little children, guard yourselves from the images of gods which lack this life. AMEN. (1Jn 5:19–21)

It is this 'penetrating mind' that we are here trying to cultivate with John.

First comes the stark polarity of good and evil with nothing in between; but then there is the suggestion that truth mediated by Christ *is* a middle position, guiding the way between these opposites. It is then indicated that Christ actually *is* this mediating position, and that he not only helps our mind to find this truth but to be one with it 'in' him. He is our middle position and we find that middle position as we find him. Moreover, this is the progressive nature of God: his position shifts from being but one pole of the world-order to one that embraces both poles; and in so doing he also embraces time and the rest of our experience. We have progressed from the idea of the divine as being transcendent to one of ever-changing relationship, and from the good-evil polarity of earlier religious outlooks to a trinitarian one that represents development and evolution in company with the divine.

The opposite of this is not evil as such but the absence of any dynamic spirituality in our lives, which can then only stagnate. Modern anthroposophy (as well as parts of modern psychology) portrays the polarity not as that of good and evil, but the evil that cramps and hardens in contrast to the evil that either dissolves or over-personalises. This is depicted in the archangel Michael holding the balance – a picture that in physics would be called dynamic equilibrium (as distinct from the static equilibrium that we so often long for but which ends up as, well, static). This is a potential difficulty we can watch for in some of the religions and customs we meet in modern life.

We can only act freely by finding, indeed by creating, the balance between these extremes. John lets us learn that it is Christ the 'mediator and advocate' who meets our efforts here and helps us continually move on.

John constructs his doctrine in stages, each of which portrays an aspect of fellowship. He has developed his own vocabulary for the new insights that he received through his closeness to Jesus in life, through being raised from the dead and through his apocalyptic revelation. So let us work through these stages where John himself begins. Each step enhances what went before. The comments are meant more as stimuli for our thoughts than as explanations.

If we then say we have fellowship with him and yet are walking in the dark, we speak a lie and are not practising truth (1Jn 1:6).

Fellowship requires light, which is bestowed by practising truth, in order to illuminate it.

But whoever keeps his word, truly God's love has been made perfect in him. Through this we know that we have our being in him. (1Jn 2:5).

It is love, proclaimed through 'his word' that links us to the divine, in an active process which brings God's love a stage further through its becoming real within us. This connects our being with his being. The prologue of John's Gospel speaks of life and light. Love only comes in later: it is still to be developed. Light enters evolution very early on, then life. Love is the desired fruit of earth evolution.

Whoever says he dwells in him will also want to walk in the way that he walked (1Jn 2:6).

This connection (dwelling, abiding) through love stimulates us to 'walk with him', an action that puts something into the world that was not there before. It is a process akin to that of transubstantiation and *active* engagement with Christ within the medium of his substance.

Let what you heard from the spirit of new beginning prepare in you an abiding place for future communion. If what you heard from the beginning does become such an abode in you, you will abide there in communion with both the Son and the Father. And this is the Spirit-word he promised us: life beyond cycles of time. (1Jn 2:24f).

Here Son and Father are both cited, going beyond just 'God'. It prepares a place within us that is a further development of the previously quoted verse (1Jn 2:6). There is this kind of communion that manifests a relationship, an abiding, and leads to a transcending of the material and temporal world.

If you realise that he bears in himself God's straight light of being, realise also that whoever works out of this light in his own being has been born out of him (1Jn 2:29).

Out of the 'abiding communion' comes a birth from God, brought about through light. This links with *righteousness* (see section in Chapter 5 where it is seen as a divine attribute that can be passed on to one's descendants).

Whoever is begotten of God does not miss his aim in his doings, because his seed abides in him and he cannot sin because he is conceived of God (1Jn 3:9).

This newly-created heredity works positively against inherited sin, or the 'sickness of sin' (as worded in the Creed in The Christian Community) and hence against all moral failings and missed aims.

And this is his spirit aim: that we should open a heart-relationship with the Name* of his Son Jesus Christ and love one another according to the aim he gave us in spirit. He who

---

* Here and in 3Jn 7 and 15 the word Name is translated with the sense that it is the appellation of the divine, archetypal 'I' Christ.

keeps this aim abides in him; and he in him. Through this we know that he is building a new soul in us, out of the spirit he has given to us. (1Jn 3:23f).
Christ's love generates love in return, through our 'I' (Name). The 'aim' is also the process of achieving it: to love. Seen like this, love does not depend upon anything. It has no cause or reason: it is past, present and future at the same time, like the divine I AM, living and moving. This generates a new soul within or around the one we had, in which the seed of God has now been sown. Put another way, our soul is transformed through our higher 'I' or ego becoming loving and takes on a quality that does not decay in death but lasts, *abides:* Spirit Self or *manas.* This is one of the principles of the human being that does not disperse after death but is retained for the future. This is how Christianity acts as an evolutionary principle as well as a confession, for the love under discussion here has a transforming, resurrecting power, the attribute of 'ego' in its selfless form as the spiritual kernel of our soul, that steers it through life.

Beloved, let us love each other because love is of God and all who love are born of God and know God (1Jn 4:7).
Through lack of love, we can, like Cain, slay each other; so now we can love each other. Love is no more just between us and God. It works around rather than directly, creating a community that understands God through experience and its fruits, in harmony with the picture of the vine and branches (Jn 15). Gradually we move in our personal theology from articles of faith to facts of experience.

God's love was shown forth in us in this, that God sent his once-born Son into the world so that we could live through him (1Jn 4:9).

Here is revealed the divine plan behind the Incarnation. The sending of the 'Son born in eternity' (a phrase from the Creed of The Christian Community) is the archetype and channel of God sending his seed into us in order to overcome death for humankind. (Without the Fall, we could not have made the free choice to overcome death through the Redeemer).

If we love one another, God makes his dwelling in us, [unfolding the members of his being in our being] and his love is brought to perfection in us (1Jn 4:12).

This rendering, including the insertion, indicates that 'dwelling' (see comment to 3:23f above) develops our higher nature further still, 'to perfection'.

Whoever confesses that Jesus is the Son of God, God weaves his soul into him and his in God. We also have received God's love into the ways of our minds and hearts. God is love and whoever builds his future soul-life through love abides in God and God abides in him.

For this, love has been brought to perfection in us, that in the day of the parting of the ways we may have confidence that we stand in the world just as he does. (1Jn 4:15–17).

The previous point is enhanced: love creates a soul that is within God and at the same time contains God. We have to enter a space other than three dimensions to experience this reality. We have to enter contemplation, meditation, prayer: then we are in the world of soul, then spirit. The 'parting of the ways' is so evident in the present time.

Everyone who believes that Jesus is the Christ, the Messiah, is begotten of God and everyone loving the begetter also loves the begotten.

We know that we love the children of God whenever we love God himself and work towards his task for us in spirit. For this is God's love: that we keep to his spiritual tasks; and these tasks are not burdensome because everything born of God vanquishes the world; and this is the victory that vanquishes the world – [the power that develops in our heart when we are relating to Jesus Christ,] our power of faith. And who can vanquish the world if not he who believes that Jesus is the Son of God? (1Jn 5:1–5).

The picture now grows by acknowledging Christ as the Messiah who will 'overcome the world'. This is special because it unites a *reality* with its own *idea* within our own cognisance. That is how we know something. In Steiner's studies of 'knowing', this union of idea and reality is seen as our 'true communion'.

And we are one with the being of truth and his Son Jesus Christ (1Jn 5:20).

This takes us back to the beginning of this exploration, to John's aim to bestow Christ's own aim, given him by the Father, to spread the word and deed of love.

The final words 'guard yourselves from the images of gods which lack this life' may refer to the ancient practice of temple servants manipulating wires so that the 'idol', the image of the god, would appear to speak and eat, to simulate what would have been the once real clairvoyant experience of the presence of the deity itself. John's Letters help us forward from a fellowship in imagination to one of real spiritual experience.

4

John's Approach to Knowing

How do we know that we do know what we think we know? There is a whole branch of philosophy about this and it plays into the balance between faith and knowledge. Do we just believe or can we prove it? To defend what we believe, we often say, 'I just *know* it!' Here, we begin to be aware that the heart does indeed have a faculty of perception and knowing, although one obviously needs much care and self-knowledge to keep straight. Faith and knowledge can be equally convincing; but what means are appropriate to each of the two spheres? Is there a way to connect the two?

To solve these life-questions, John took a special approach; for even a logical proof within the material world is sometimes open to question. Take cause and effect, for example. In some instances it is clear: the cause of a vessel breaking is that it was dropped and the floor was too hard for it to withstand the blow. But what was the cause of my missing the bus? Missing the bus made it possible for an important encounter to occur instead of what I had planned. That 'unplanned' encounter is also a cause: it caused me subconsciously (in my will) to be preoccupied and so delayed. The cause operated out of the future.

How does John lead us into a knowledge that is above this level of cause and effect? He works with inner experience rather than external information, for it is within our own soul that we can tell whether we are on the right path to grasping something. This is only just being recognised by modern thought. John shares his experiences to let us encounter existentially the spiritual being of Christ, along with the Father and the Spirit, but as one. He achieves this by taking a particular motif and expressing it in different ways, gradually developing a flow of images till the whole is manifested. The method enables us to perceive more deeply than the senses alone can, just as we perceive on a deeper level the whole melody lying beyond the different tones and intervals the ear can actually hear. It is grasped directly within the soul.

Here is an example, with some indications. The phrase 'by this we know', or one of its variants, introduces little cameos throughout the Letters, which, in themselves, seem not to say anything logical, but taken as a whole create a spiritual figure that we can inwardly begin to comprehend at a level higher than our mind or intellect. He introduces us to aspects of the Godhead as a being with whom we can relate rather than as something transcendent. The comments are but aphoristic hints, since it is difficult to improve on our own pondering. In this way we move from intellectual clarity into the poetic word picture, then into the depths of *being*.

Knowing is thus felt to be a connection to the *being* of something. It is a deed rather than a reflection.

This is how we know that we have known him: that we keep to the aim he sets before our spirit (1Jn 2:3).

This sentence seems to prove something, yet not in the normal way. Knowing must mean following a direction set before us; that is, doing something. This knowledge is born out of our will and perceived by it.

But whoever keeps his word, truly God's love has been made perfect in him. Through this we know that we have our being in him. (1Jn 2:5).

This likewise hardly follows, yet *keep* can also here just mean being an extension of God through his word – hence we *know*, as it has become *our* word too.

Through this we know the nature of love, that he spread his living soul over us (1Jn 3:16).

If one ponders this sentence for a while, one feels included in his love, his soul spread over us like an embracing, empowering mantel; and one wants to share it with others.

... let us not love in word or in speech but in deeds and within the living truth of the congregation. In this way we shall know ourselves to be part of the living spirit of true community. (1Jn 3:18f).

Through action – once again though our will – we 'know' on a life-level instead of just in the head. These Letters are after all about 'the Word of Life'.

He who keeps this aim abides in him; and he in him. Through this we know that he is building a new soul in us. (1Jn 3:24).

The abiding can be sensed because our inner development can be sensed. The barrier between ourselves and the world, which we had to erect as toddlers to hold our

'I' intact, now needs to come down so that we can be in communion with what is outside us. The abiding soul of Christ contains both us and the others, so there is no danger of losing our self.

Through this we know that our future soul-life is woven in him and his in us: he has given us of his spirit-breath (1Jn 4:13).

In the moment we feel God loving others *through us* as 'spirit breath' we know we are woven together. This links to the later description in John's Gospel of Easter evening (20:22), 'He breathed on them and said "Receive holy breath".' (The same Greek word is used for both breath and spirit). This indicates a kind of sharing of soul between the resurrected Christ and those human beings seeking him.

We know that we love the children of God whenever we love God himself and work towards his task for us in spirit (1Jn 5:2).

Here is a strange thing: by loving God we know we love those born of him. That is something that will not often occur to us.

In conclusion there are three things we are allowed merely to know, without the 'through this', simply as existential facts not requiring causes. These are the fruits of what went before and may indicate to us that the process might need to be repeated, possibly regularly.

We know that everyone begotten of God does not sin (1Jn 5:18).

We know that we are of God (1Jn 5:19).

We know that the Son of God has come ... [and led us to the spirit] (1Jn 5:20).

The three members of the Trinity can here be recognised: the begetter as the Father; the one who helps us stay connected as the Son; and the one who leads us ever onwards as the Spirit.

It is this exalted piece of knowledge, which embraces both sober confession and devout belief, that John reveals to us through this series of observations, as they move together within our soul and awaken our spirit to 'God'.

Then we are aware of how John *knows*. He 'knows' the living relationship between God and humanity. His knowing is at once fellowship, and includes his listeners.

With these fruits we can now turn to selected words.

5

Significant Words

Abide

Rendered as abide or dwell

The reader of the King James (or Authorised) Version of the Bible may still love this word, but wonder at its continuing use here – it is perhaps a slightly archaic memory of an earlier age expressed in hymns. Its functioning as the catalyst for this work was described in the Introduction. For a translation it has the virtue of providing both verb and noun: abide and abode. The alternatives, *continue, remain* and *dwell,* cannot do this, although 'dwelling' is near. 'Lodge' does have this possibility, as a sacred dwelling but calls up the domestic connotations of 'lodging' or the secrecy of a Masonic Lodge, giving a different though not totally inaccurate association. *Dwell* is used in this translation where it fits better than abide, but the phrases 'abiding place', 'abiding presence' would not work with dwell. Abide also has the positive connotation of duration.

The Greek word behind all these is *menein,* to dwell or abide. Its loveliest context is in the Gospel, 'If anyone loves me he will keep my word and my Father will love him and we shall come to him and abide with him' (Jn 14:23). The image is dynamic yet gentle, bearing the prospect of a total change in our lives. It is introduced already in Chapter 1, 'Master, where are you abiding?'... 'Come and see' (Jn 1:38f). This is brought to a beautiful conclusion at Emmaus, 'Abide with us, for it is towards evening and the day is now far spent' (Lk 24:29).

Menein has the same root as *man* and *manas* and this fact has guided the translation. *Manas,* used by Steiner in the theosophical context, with oriental nomenclature, is that member of our whole being we are next to develop, through bringing our soul life under the rulership of our 'I', rather than have our personal ideas, impulses and feelings decide for us how we should behave. He called it Spirit Self (see pp. 50), the ordinary, provisional self that has been developed and spiritualised. Through the work done on the soul (a work not to be underestimated!) the transformed part will not dissolve away after death but 'remain', abide. Jesus uses this word in this sense about John: 'If he abide until I come, what is that to you?' (Jn 21:23).

So what has 'abide' or 'dwell' to do with our development? What can come about through the abiding? Some of the renderings in the translation that seek to answer this may appear far-fetched, but they are chosen to allow the full meaning to emerge.

The essential ingredient of the development of Spirit Self is the transcending and overcoming of the self-assertive and selfish 'I', raising it out of the realm of sympathy and antipathy to become a free director of our soul. It is the charioteer (Phaedrus), to borrow Plato's image. The soul's egotism can only be truly ordered in a social context (love your neighbour as yourself), so the word used by Jesus amongst the disciples indicates a catalyst in a social or communal context. 'He who abides in me and I abide in him, he bears much fruit' (Jn 15:5), or in the passage from John 15 quoted later in the essay on love:

'as the Father has loved me so have I loved you: abide in my love'. And the Comforter may 'abide with you for ever...You know him for he abides with you and will be in you' (Jn 14:16f).

In this context, then, abiding or dwelling indicates the essential characteristic of a community. Jesus is experiencing himself as the place where all the powers of the Trinity are focussing as he establishes the first Christian community of the disciples. John, as the beloved disciple, has had immediate access to this communion and is at pains to transmit this experience to the subsequent Christian Communities that are to be images of it.

When the Christ, the Father and the Spirit can abide in the congregation – through the righteousness of the Father, the love of the Son and the truth of the Healing Spirit – then that congregation is a place where the Spirit Self is developed by our *individual* striving meeting a *communal* Christian grace. A congregation, or comparable group striving for a spiritual purpose around Christianity as an evolutionary force, works at this often without realising it. Much of the work is caused by collaborating to keep a church or religious group together. Personalities come into closer contact because of the nearness of the spiritual world than they otherwise would 'at work'.

It is surprising what goes on, and is resolved, out of public view in this arena. This provides both the ferment we need in our attempts at co-operating and the powers required to deal with their consequences, whereas in other areas of modern life the ferment is often provided by worldly impulses that do not offer anything of the blessing of the higher power that is available in a Christian congregation. The fallen nature of humanity is primarily to be seen as the cramping of the 'I' or spirit into the soul. This brings the 'I' too much under the sway of the soul's likes and dislikes but also makes the soul self-seeking. Coming together in a soul-spiritual context whose purpose is to maintain a spiritual activity for its own sake is already an activity whose nature is super-personal and raises the 'I' out of the soul into its own sovereignty. It also brings souls together in a non-competitive way where they learn to serve the whole and benefit from its blessings. *Abiding* together develops the Spirit Self as a gift of the Holy Spirit, through its warm, incubating (brooding) power.

We sometimes cannot abide something or someone. We cannot bear them in our 'space'. This negative gives the clue to the positive, to create through goodwill a new space that is able to include us both. In John's light, this space may also be a dwelling for the divine, actively enhancing our effort to transform 'abide' from an outdated relic of old forms into the gentle beginnings of a new spiritual journey.

The rendering of *menein* and its derivatives in these Letters tries to bring out this element.

Righteousness

Rendered as 'the good straight light of God'
It was understood by ancient wisdom that the noblest human qualities came from God. In ancient Egypt the goddess Maat bestowed those qualities, imbuing relationships with divine order: harmony, life, fruitfulness, justice and *righteousness*. The soul filled with Maat was, at death, light as a feather (her crown carries an upright feather) and straight as the light. Yet Maat was not a primal divinity but the offspring of the Sun being Ra (or Re), and was also what nourished Ra as he indwelt the Pharaoh. Her quality as a living being was then like the Logos or the Word proceeding from the Godhead, later described by John in the prologue of the Gospel. In the New Kingdom, however, we see that the use of Maat in the

royal name is more a personal claim than an inner experience, for these were kings of external power: Seti I *(Menmaat-Ra,* abiding in God's righteousness) and Rameses II *(User-maat-Ra,* powerful in God's righteousness), two pharaohs living about the time of Moses.* Righteousness, however, has nowadays become a legalistic term and lost some of its original virtue, which needs restoring.

In the Old Testament it is the figure of Abraham who is deemed righteous. Righteousness was his moral warmth and light of faith that made a bridge between him and Yahweh (Rm 4:3, Gn 15:6: 'Abraham believed God and it was counted to him as righteousness'). He felt there was no life worth living without this bridge of spirit warmth over which the light of the divine 'I' could visit him: 'Here am I.' This was a real relationship, tangible in warmth of being and upright devoutness, more dear to him than his own long-promised son. This Logos manifests again through Moses as he sits all day in judgment over the people, 'straightening' their problems. But because the Israelites generally lacked this faculty of flexible judgment at that time, the living and life-giving Logos-Maat had to be entombed in the law. The Ten Commandments, and the many other detailed laws that covered the whole of life, were needed to replace the lost inner sense of the good straight light of God. This law had to be imposed instead of being inwardly 'divined'.

In our time the development of moral awareness as distinct from following commandments or edicts demonstrates a fresh acquisition of this quality. Where it is completely lacking, we have severe social difficulties.

---

* The additional royal names of the Pharaohs are found on the Saqqara Tablet in the Egyptian Museum in Cairo. Shelley's 'Ozymandias' is an anglicising of User-maat-Ra, the Pharaoh Rameses II (reigned 1279–1213 BC). The poem portrays the downfall that ensues when true righteousness is lost.

'For your hardness of heart he wrote you this commandment' (Mk 10:5). The righteousness that had been
a moral warmth and light in Abraham became, under
the law, externally legalistic. Paul indeed holds the law
responsible for sin, 'under a curse' (Gal 3:10). Through
it, one became justified (or straightened) before the
court, just as one had hoped to be justified at death by
a life righteous before the law in Egyptian times. This
enabled Abraham to be the ancestor of a nation in which
the ultimate bringer to humanity of the Logos–Maat
quality, or substance could be born. 'The promise to
Abraham *and his descendants,* that they should inherit the
world, did not come through the law but through the
righteousness of faith' (Rm 4:13). Paul wants to make
it clear that righteousness is a quality acquired through
faith that becomes an inner moral power. He indicates
that although righteousness begins as a personal moral
force, it is also transmitted to descendants through the
blood (a difficult idea for the modern mind), counter-
ing the inherited fallen nature and laying a foundation
for people to develop further righteousness themselves
(1Jn 2:29).

In this way it works for the overcoming of the sickness of sin of man's *bodily* nature (as the Creed in The
Christian Community states). Paul adds the contrast, that
where there is no law there is no transgression. He does
not want anarchy (literally, 'without rulership') but the
rulership of Maat, the inner Logos or I AM.

Four New Testament figures stand before us in the
'good straight light of God': the aged Zechariah and
Elizabeth ('both righteous before God', Lk 1:6) whose
lives enhanced Abraham's legacy and passed it on to
their son John the Baptist; Joseph, the father of Jesus,
who refused to expose Mary's pregnancy (Mt 1:19); and
Simeon who could hear the Spirit directing him to the

temple to receive and bless the holy family (Lk 2:25). All act out of their own morality instead of merely out of the law. All play their part in paving the way for Christ, who, in uniting with Jesus, was to lift fallen Maat again to Logos, lift the law again to grace and truth (Jn 1:17).

Righteousness is the relationship that passes to humanity from God through the Son, the mediator and advocate (1Jn 2:1). It is an essence that works with one's own will and feeling rather than the logic of the mind. Right is straight like light (or rather the boundary between light and shadow) and good like warmth: 'no one is good but God alone' (Mk 10:18) – hence 'the good straight light of God', which draws us up as straight as Joseph's staff, warm as Simeon's heart, steadfast as Elizabeth and Zechariah; our soul becomes as light as the feather of Maat.

John reports Jesus as saying that the Holy Spirit, the Advocate, will come and convince the world about righteousness because he is going to the Father, out of our sight (16:8). We are free now. He does not impose righteousness, as some would have us believe, but through his Spirit lets us draw it from him. Finally, Jesus' prayer to the Father closes with the address, 'O righteous Father' (17:25). He, Jesus the man, looks through his Christness to the source or Father of righteousness, the origin of Logos and Maat: God the Father. God's warm light through Christ enters humanity in Jesus. This warmth carries him into and through death as a new inheritance. This light prepares us to receive the risen Christ – not as Ra indwelt the Pharaoh but born in us of the Father, freely to bring life and order to humankind and the world. The righteous Father begets a righteous Son to become both the new ancestor and the brother of the modern human being.

Love

How did John become the one able to witness Christ in those last hours when he taught those present how to love? Is there anything that also could help *us* enter into this mystery?

The gospel account of what follows after the final meal and conversation with his closest followers (the Last Supper) covers four chapters out of twenty-one. They contain descriptions of actions, words, questions and many delicate and intimate images. They challenge both our comprehension and our ability to accept. They begin by telling us what Jesus was thinking. How does John know that? Later Peter asks what Jesus meant about the betrayal. Lazarus-John knows. There are long passages not reported elsewhere. We at first only guess that John means Lazarus (see Introduction), 'the disciple whom Jesus loved', when describing that he 'leant on the breast of Jesus' (Jn 13:23). Later he is explicit; but what sort of experience would that be? We would feel warmth – the warmth of the Messiah, or 'Christ', the anointed one of God. We would feel the breath that had spoken I AM, had spoken 'the Word' that had created 'all things' (Jn 1:3). We would have felt the heartbeat that sustains the life of the universe. And alongside all this we would understand the betrayal, we would feel the thoughts, emotions and concerns of the one who had raised us from the dead.

Such feelings help us grasp the inner substance of these chapters, for this theme, the substance of *love,* particularly as it is portrayed in Chapter 15 of John's Gospel, is the most important of all Christ's teachings and deeds. It permeates all John's writings. Pondering and meditating John's sensations, perceptions and divinations as he leaned there, opens for us the way to loving and being loved to the point where we can feel something that transcends living and dying. We sense a breath of immortality.

What happens when we try to realise this in our own lives? The following may help in this. It is to do with relationships.

Amongst the many themes covered, Jesus spoke in detail about his connection to the Father and to the Spirit, as three and as one. He also spoke about his relationship to us in a moving way, in particular about love:

> As the Father has loved me so have I loved you: abide in my love. If you keep before you the aim I give you, you will abide in my love, as I have kept before me the aim given me by my Father and abide in his love. This is the aim I have set before you, that you love one another in the way that I have loved you. No-one has greater love than this, that he lay down the life of his soul for his friends. You are my friends if you work for the aim that I myself set before you. (Jn 15:9–14)

It is just possible that we can sense the feeling expressed in the words of an Irish blessing, 'May God hold you in the palm of his hand,' for these chapters are composed of pictures of God raying himself down upon his Son, in righteousness, truth and love, to abide there. The Son's mission is to bring these gifts of divine-cosmic magnitude further down to humanity so that we can engage with them and raise ourselves up to our full stature. Father to Son to human beings: the flow of love reaches *us* at this meal. The beloved disciple opens himself to us so that we too can become beloved disciples. He mediates between us and Christ, as Christ does between the disciples – particularly John – and the Father. It is the mystery of death and resurrection that is the key to this mediation. We are in God's hand, but sent out freely, out of our own initiative, and hence upon our own authority. We carry his magic, like a fairy tale whose heroines and heroes have had mystery gifts bestowed upon them that will be just right for the moments of destiny they are bound to meet. Death and resurrection is the outer appearance of love, and we need that in order to love, with our true 'I', yet without too much *self*. This mood would have permeated the ceremonial meals that commemorated this in the early church, the *agapē* or love-meal, the 'love-sacrifice' of Chapter 2 of the First Letter.

But what about love for another person, 'personally' rather than in this divine-ideal sense of the word? One might want to say, 'Why make it so complex? Loving is easy.' We say as easy as falling off a log; gravity does it for us. So with falling in love: the depths of our soul do it for us – and give us one of the most powerful experiences possible. We cease to be interested in self-control or freedom. But what if we are dumped or betrayed? Then a vivid impression is gained of the need to free our self from what is happening in our soul. Even with a free 'I' over against our soul, it is like performing heart surgery on our self.

Did we feel 'I need you'? What is this need if not just one half of a relationship? Was I also needed, and now feel that loss? A very large proportion of human creativity and output stems from these conditions and forces. What we are seeing is that our self has been caught up too deeply in the soul, making it fettered, and the soul has grasped at the 'I' too tightly, making it selfish. (see 'Abide' above).

A lovely image of balance in personal love is expressed by Sir Philip Sidney, 'My True Love Hath My Heart':

My true-love hath my heart, and I have his,
By just exchange, one for the other given:
I hold his dear, and mine he cannot miss;
There never was a better bargain driven.
His heart in me keeps me and him in one;
My heart in him his thoughts and senses guides:
He loves my heart, for once it was his own;
I cherish his, because in me it bides.
His heart his wound received from my sight:
My heart was wounded with his wounded heart;
For as from me on him his hurt did light,
So still, methought, in me his hurt did smart:
Both equal hurt, in this change sought our bliss:
My true-love hath my heart and I have his.

It joins up several of the themes around raising love to
its home without losing its intensity. The hearts are inside
each other, something not of three-dimensional, earthly
space, but only possible in soul space, like I in God and
God in me. We saw the importance of the heart as the
organ of faith and the place, the abode, for the spirit, and
now, for other people too.

What makes the poem all the more poignant is that
it is spoken by a shepherdess to her beloved cradled in
her lap. Although he is not dead, the scene is a pieta, a
motif from the Holy Grail, and it is the mutual healing
of their mutual wounds that is the fruit of their love. The
lines about the wounds are omitted in some publications
but taken to their extreme they touch Christ's words in
the Sermon on the Mount (Mt 5:44, Lk 6:27), 'love your
enemies'. That really demonstrates the sovereignty of the
Christ-inspired human 'I' over and within the soul. It
reveals that *agapē* has taken its place alongside attraction
and devotion, elevating them all. It values the other as
itself, neither selfish nor self-less. It depicts in an earthly

scene what John aims to tell of our possibilities with the Father and the Son, to work the Spirit within us.

One thinks of hate being the opposite of love, but John presents another: fear. Our age seems to be the epoch of fear. Fear is so all-pervasive that most of us have no idea how far we have slid into it as a way of life. We may fall in with authority to avoid threats, but the fear drives itself ever deeper with the aid of so much of modern culture and media presentations because there is nothing to dissolve it away. Fear 'sells' well because it lives deep down in everyone, along with a couple of other emotions. We are at home with it and subconsciously feel it is important for everyone yet it makes us isolated. Even in a crowd, it is our *own* fear. This is an evolutionary situation so we can gain in spiritual stature as we learn to master it; and John offers the way. 'There is no fear in love, but love casts out fear as it is perfected' (1Jn 4:18). 'As it is perfected'; so it is a process, the process outlined here. It takes time and perseverance but there we are not alone.

Love is, after all, the aim of Christianity for changing earth evolution through humanity, and to show that is John's prime task in these Letters.

Truth

Pilate's famous words, 'What is truth?' occur in the brief discussion with Jesus about his kingship: 'For this I have been born and for this I have come into the world, to bear witness to the truth' (Jn 18:37). However, prior to this, after the Last Supper, he has already told Thomas, 'I AM the way and the *truth* and the life. No-one comes to the Father but by me.' This aspect of truth, as something leading to the Father, is one which can link it to righteousness. They both belong to the divine order: they come from the Father. But also coming from the Father is Christ: 'I proceeded from the Father and have entered the world; now I am leaving the world and going on to the Father' (Jn 16:28). Christ brings truth from the Father, and Jesus carries it through death. In bearing it back to the Father, the Spirit can be sent: 'The Father shall give you another Comforter, that he may abide with you for ever, the Spirit of Truth' (Jn 14:16); 'unless I go, the Comforter (or spirit guide, or helper) will not come; but if I do go, I shall send him to you' (Jn 16:7).

This is the picture that overshines John's Letters, that this truth comes from now on not from the Father – the past – but from the Spirit, from the future, beyond death. And this spirit of truthfulness 'abides' with the congregation, if it lives aright (that is, in righteousness). And the truth does not bind itself to a law – it makes one free, 'free indeed' ('if the Son makes you free, you will be free indeed,' Jn 8:36).

The rendering of the Letters here shows this connection between truth and the Holy Spirit. Insofar as truth abides within the congregation, it is related to the spirit of the community. The spirit of a Christian congregation is like an angelic servant, like a limb of Christ himself, within the weaving of love. There is a hint of this in the Apocalypse, where Christ's letters are to go to the 'angel of the church' of Ephesus, etc. even though delivered into a human hand, possibly the priest. The bonding of such congregations into real communities is under the incubating warmth-power of the Holy Spirit. Truth is not just the legalistic opposite of falsehood: it is that which lifts our spirit into a spiritual world that is harmonious in itself. There it is a life principle. The prologue of John's Gospel says, 'for the law was given through Moses; grace and truth came through Jesus Christ' (1:17). The substance of the spirit world can be felt to be a rarefied form of thought-substance and it is through thinking, backed up by a mood of prayer, that we penetrate into that world: 'The Spirit of Truth will guide you into the whole truth' (Jn 16:13) and the Son prays the Father to 'Consecrate them in your truth: your Word is truth' (Jn 17:17). Is not this a wonderfully compact expression of the unity of the Trinity: the Father, the Son or Word, and the Spirit of Truth?

For most people, the idea that the spiritual world is made up of thought-substance is hard to approach. Thoughts are in our head while the spirit world is out or up 'there', if it exists at all. But consider: we have everyday thoughts, from the mundane to the sublime, but they are usually still to do with earthly matters. However, we can extract general thoughts from them and arrive at concepts of wider import, unaffected by the turmoil of the world. These can in turn acquire the quality of the eternal, rising freely above the ephemeral. They are still thoughts but have become, through our inner activity, *universal* ones. In thinking them we can feel our own thought life to be connected to that of the eternal. We no longer feel we have created them ourselves but that in thinking them we are allowing a place in our own spirit for them to make themselves conscious here upon earth. We have reached into the world of spirit, just by touching it with our thoughts. This is, of course, not a proof but rather a pointer to the way one can experience the idea that the spiritual world is of the same substance as thought, but living thought, capable of acting as something alive, within one's own soul. Steiner characterises this process: through bringing together our whole thought life into a unified whole 'We feel that we have the truth.'* John's writings contain such eternal thoughts.

A consecration of humanity in truth unites us already in the present with that which will give us life and light

* 'The Inner Nature of Thinking', p. 40, *Goethe's Theory of Knowledge* (CW 2) SteinerBooks, USA 2008.

in the world of truth, the spiritual world, and hence the life after death. The Letters culminate in a picture of truth (3Jn 3 and 12) as a *place* (the community) – 'see the place where they laid him' (Mt 28:6; Mk 16:6) – encompassing both the earthly world of a Christian community and the higher world of the spirit. Within this we grow inwardly as individuals and outwardly as members of humanity.

It is then sometimes helpful, in context, that 'truth' be rendered: 'true spirit of the community'.

Grace

In the Second Letter this word begins a triad: 'Grace, mercy and peace are to be with us through God the Father and through Jesus Christ the Son of the Father in the light of this truth and the warmth of this love' (2Jn 3). We are usually confident that we understand truth and have a reasonable idea of mercy; but grace is less clear. Usages are difficult to combine into an overall meaning: grace before meals and gracious movement, even 'gracious majesty', although the latter might be nearer the primal meaning, since kingship is an earthly representative of spiritual powers, as the royal crown suggests. Grace emerges when our physical surroundings are ordered and we bear ourselves gracefully. When bread seems to shine to the housekeeper out of the gracious devotion put into its preparation, it has been brought to a stage towards the bread of communion. Those who can sense this imaginatively are also on their way to seein a shining aura around the altar bread. We have taken a step in developing Spirit Man, where the bodily realm is permeated, as in consecrated bread (for 'Spirit Man' see pp. 50f).

Following the quest to derive John's vocabulary from his usage, we note that this is the only occurrence of grace in the Letters. We must conclude that for John, grace belongs with mercy and peace and the three together suggest a possible link to the Trinity, as did righteousness, love and truth.

But a significant use occurs in the prologue of John's Gospel, as mentioned above under 'Truth', namely, 'For the law was given through Moses; *grace* and truth came through Jesus Christ' (Jn 1:17). Here we can picture the law from Yahweh as guidance for people's lives but also as a contract: if you keep my law I will ensure that you prosper. Many Old Testament stories relate the woes that afflicted the people when they defaulted on this agreement, suffering defeat or plague as a consequence. The law described the relationship between God and humanity. Now it is in grace and truth where that relationship is to be found.

Grace is English for *charis,* meaning grace, kindness, and life. The King James translation of St Paul reads, 'And now abideth faith, hope, *charity,* these three; but the greatest of these is *charity'* (1Cor 13:13). However, the Greek word that is translated as charity is not *charis,* but *agapē,* love. So love is also added to grace's attributes through this quirk of inspired translation from the early seventeenth century that used 'charity' where we now use 'love'. Note 'abideth' here too, indicating that Paul's three primary Christian virtues also relate to the development of the Spirit Self. Christianity is the new mystery, fostering traditional spiritual development in a way that has now been transformed by the resurrection and opened up to the wider associations of our everyday lives.

The Graces in Greek tradition were also called the 'charities' and brought charm, beauty, nature, human creativity and fertility to humankind, that is, the qualities of the divine female. Although Charis seems to have been but one of the minor graces, her name is used for them collectively. John has therefore seen that Christianity has raised this divine-feminine quality to greater significance, in contrast with the male orientation of Yahweh the law-giver.

Grace has a feeling of movement, not as fixed as the law. As well as depicting a beautiful motion, 'gracious' implies being flexible with laws; and bearing in mind the quotation from Paul that sin is a consequence of the law, we see how important grace is in helping us through our moral maze without being too crippled by the harmful results of poor decisions. In Old Testament days we could have known the consequences of lawlessness – and in the world of modern law we still can, even though the sentences are in the hands of judges. But we cannot now know how the divine world will react to our moral deeds. That is a secret that Grace keeps to herself! We have to develop an eye, a feeling for the working of grace. In general we might say, as a starting hypothesis, that everything good that comes to us is grace, every success is grace, rather than being due to our own prowess. Such an attitude frees our 'I' from the soul. Failures and blows of fate can on the other hand be taken as challenges – divine prompts us to develop a stronger 'I': 'whom God loves, he also chastens' is an oft recurring theme. That is also grace.

We experience more peace in life, and life's truths become a little more transparent, because we are not holding fast to our own idea of how life should be. It is ancient wisdom that this positive renunciation of our own will actually helps the good to come about. It does not mean that we renounce concern but open ourselves to an outcome of greater wisdom than ours. We just need to see it from someone else's perspective, even a divine one.

For grace to visit, the spiritual world needs to be addressed. Prayer is the way to do this. Prayer makes the things prayed for more visible to the eye of heaven because we have dressed them in the light and warmth of our own human insight and caring. Then we may picture divine grace as a flow that assists God's blessing to reach us through Christ, finding the best place to touch the earth in order to bring the greatest fruitfulness to our common destiny. In the communion service of The Christian Community, the picture is that grace descends in response to the incense of prayer. This seems right.

It is a grace to be granted insight into the working of grace.

Mercy

Mercy mediates Christ's 'healing oil', which helps or oils all aspects of relationships and destinies, expressed in the fruits of the true vine and in the communion of wine. Mercy as oil is seen in the parable of the Good Samaritan (Lk 10:29–37), and 'the oil of mercy' is what Seth, in a legend, seeks of the Cherubic guardian of heaven for his dying father, Adam.

Like grace, this word also occurs only once, in the same place as the other two, ('Grace, *mercy* and peace are to be with us through God the Father and through Jesus Christ the Son of the Father,' 2Jn 3). It is not as frequent a word as peace. It is more to be found in the Old Testament, notably in the description of the Ark of the Covenant – again a connection to the law. Mercy is God's prerogative not to apply the consequence of the law. The law is not replaced, as through Jesus Christ, with grace and truth; it is simply withheld. Part of the construction of the ark was the 'mercy seat', an extraordinary creation of two solid gold Cherubim facing each other, the wings outstretched in front of them, just touching those of the other, creating a space within (Ex 25:17–20). The whole was placed upon the top of the ark in the Holy of Holies of the tent of meeting; and when Moses came to speak with Yahweh, he sat at the side of the ark before this space. God appeared to him in radiance and conversed with him from the other side. Moses afterwards had to cover his face as the divine light that had shone upon it remained and was too dazzling for the people to look at. This space between divine wings was thus itself a sacred object acting as the threshold to the divine world. Where the Egyptians had an *image* of the god, here there was a *space,* hinting at the space that is made within us when we have diminished our egotism and into which our higher 'I' may enter. God remained spirit. We may recall it was a Cherub who guarded this threshold against the return of Adam and Eve at their expulsion from paradise and also thereby our own return. The same beings now represent this threshold between God and Moses.

Moving on now to the New Testament and the ministry of Christ, we find that in the beatitudes of the Sermon on the Mount (Mt 5–7), mercy takes the middle position: 'Blessed are the merciful for they shall obtain mercy'. It moves from being the prerogative of the Father to that of the Son, the divine centre that engages with us mortals; a direct encounter with either the Father or the Spirit would be overwhelming for the uninitiated. Christ himself takes the place for us of the mercy seat of the Old Covenant. Mercy is unique amongst these beatitude qualities in that it moves between humanity and God in both directions, the only beatitude that is reflexive. This is the hallmark of the 'I' too, the individual self that relates us to the surrounding world outside and to the spirit within itself. The 'I' has the peculiarity of being spatially within the rest of us, yet being at the same time the point within which our spiritual dimension will open out – that is, in a *different order* of space, that opens *inwards.* Mercy stands in the centre of the beatitudes; our 'I' stands at the centre of our being, between three parts of the body (physical, ethereal and astral), and their trans-formation into Spirit Self (or *manas),* Life Spirit (*buddhi*) and Spirit Man (*atman*). Here it differs from grace in that it is *already* a human quality of preparedness to meet the divine and the divine quality of being prepared to meet us human beings. This two-way flow suggests a connection to the Son, the mediator between God and human-ity, although as so often, what applies to Christ may apply to the Spirit also. Grace, mercy and peace clearly do have some connection with Father, Son and Spirit, but we should note that everything to do with the Trinity is mobile, flowing together and should not be made into a static scheme.

How do we feel when we receive mercy? We may experience its closeness to grace, yet it can awaken us to a new destiny. We have received something that quickens in us the wish to give something out of ourselves. Grace may enable us to carry out this wish but seems to be more 'lateral', whereas mercy is directed, if one may express it in this way. Peace may result from this, in the sense that Christ's relationship to the world is one of peace.

To the English ear, 'mercy' brings to mind the speech of Portia in Shakespeare's *Merchant of Venice:*

> The quality of mercy is not strained
> It droppeth as the gentle rain from heaven
> Upon the place beneath. It is twice blessed:
> It blesseth him that *gives* and him that *takes.*

Truly inspired words, they create a dynamic picture of growth within a human soul. The speech concludes:

> It is an attribute to God himself;
> And earthly power doth then show likest God's
> When mercy seasons justice.

We are again close to the theme of the Letters, indicating how, in community, human qualities essential to our future culture may be developed through the closeness of the Spirit. Portia stands out amongst all the characters as being the one possessed of 'I' rather than just soul.

The passion with which the words 'Have mercy' may be spoken or called out, indicates its essential place in our lives – to give and to receive. It builds community.

Grace and peace support our attempts at mercy, grace in our comportment, peace in our soul.

Peace

Peace comes through 'abiding' with Christ; peace with the world is the first part of the threefold communion section in The Christian Community and the third element of that communion itself. This is Spirit Self, which develops communally in a congregation through the striving of the members within it (see 'Abide', p. 69). This may be a joint effort of like minds to achieve a common goal or it may be the older usage of 'striving', where people must wrestle with themselves and each other in order to make progress.

This is the first word spoken to the disciples by the Risen Christ on Easter evening (Jn 20:25) and is still the customary greeting of both Jews and Arabs, *shalom* and *salaam,* ever since. For us it is also a special greeting, playing the same role as the Easter greeting of some European countries, 'Christ is Risen.'

It is also the attribute of our true self, through which fear of the future can be laid aside so we can relate to the world with an even breath and quiet heart: in peace.

In our time, peace is in the news a great deal but usually for the lack of it. We seem always to be looking for it but seldom finding it. It usually means something that begins with a ceasefire that, one hopes, will continue through negotiations. This usually means a sort of bargaining and often, though not always, comes about only because of threat of force or sanctions. Meanwhile, whose hearts are at peace? Peace really has nothing to do with war; it is not the opposite of war, but an attitude. Look at epic narratives of great warriors. They had to be at peace with themselves before the battle. Of especial note here is Arjuna. His charioteer, who subsequently reveals himself as Krishna, is a kind of archangel Michael figure, quietening Arjuna's soul. Through this he is prepared to fight the battle so that the good may prevail, not to be diverted by earthly or tribal considerations.

For us too, peace is an inner condition and the prevalence of war in the world is a projection of a general lack of a peaceful centre within human lives. Neither fanaticism nor the desire for power can bring about peace, for it is they that pull the soul either to the left or the right, *taking away* its peace.

To find peace, we need a direction to follow, so that our soul is purposefully engaged. This direction needs to have such a power of attraction that it can overcome ideology and desire; the way must hold all these diversions in balance so that the one extreme is tempered by the other. This is Michael's balance in our time. So what is this direction?

John is clear that Christ's main message is that we should learn to love. Standard translations say that his 'commandment' is love. But can one love to order? Is it not rather an objective to pursue that he has given? The Letters soon reveal that this love is their central theme. John's epithet is 'There is no fear in love, for love casts out fear as it is perfected' (1Jn 4:18). It is a process, not a state. It comes and goes as we walk the path towards it. If we think we have arrived we are mistaken: it is in *pursuing* this objective that we find peace because each step into the world on that path has a purpose that makes everything else worthwhile. We find peace with the world and with ourselves at the same time. That is a discovery of our 'I'. Out of this peace we can love; and this love helps us achieve peace. Christ is given to say that his relationship to the world is to stand at *peace* with it (in The Christian Community communion service).

Verse 3 of John's Second Letter, where 'peace' occurs, says, 'grace, mercy and peace are to be with us through God the Father and through Jesus Christ, the Son of the Father, in the light of this truth and the warmth of this love.' This shows how peace may be acquired when other virtues are also practised, as portrayed in the sections on grace and mercy.

These three virtues are some of the fruits of the relationship we can have with the Trinity as it abides with us.

Commandment and sin

These are words that have turned many people away from Christianity. The need to receive moral commands from someone else is fast disappearing, except towards someone charismatic, supernatural, 'special', or in situations of emergency or the unknown. This aspect is more hidden in the modern world but efforts are certainly being made by some to 'command' others.

The word 'commandment' in the New Testament is about an aim or a goal, not an order, although Christ does give it with some emphasis. For instance: 'If I had not come and spoken to them, they would not have sin; but now they have no excuse for their sin ... If I had not done amongst them the works which no-one else did, they would not have sin; but now they have seen and hated both me and my Father' (Jn 15:22–24).

Sin here has a different connotation, meaning in Greek to miss the mark, whereas in English it is related to 'sunder', being separated. Neither is really pejorative but rather descriptive of a fact. Missing the mark connects therefore with that of commandment, to give an aim. This is clear in the First Letter, 'whoever keeps his word [to love], truly God's love has been made perfect in him' (1Jn 2:5). Commandment and perfection both contain the root referring to an aim for the future, *telos*. The 'they' in the above quotation singles out the archetypal missing of the archetypal aim, to love God.

We have already quoted Paul, that sin was the consequence of the law. One can feel that; but if the law, which was prescriptive, has now changed into the free aim to love, we cannot draw the same conclusion. 'The law was given through Moses, grace and truth came through Jesus Christ' (Jn 1:17). The aim of love can certainly be missed, indeed one may feel it to be a special achievement to love at all in Christ's sense. However, it might be better to feel it as a gift than an achievement because the fallen human being cannot 'achieve' this without the tuition and example of this 'teacher of love'. When we fail in love we simply want to try again, for that is what love does to us. It draws us ever onwards out of its own divine strength, to 'bear fruit that abides' (Jn 15:16). One usually judges oneself and sees that the failure was due to too much selfhood getting in the way. Love itself is not the aim – it is a power and beyond aim, yet Christ, through John, gives it as the ultimate aim, a force from the future to take humanity into the future. Such an aim is never *fulfilled* in earthly terms but it does transform those following it. That changes 'commandment' from its Old Testament meaning into a life force that gradually becomes perfect within. In this aim the goal 'out there' is at the same time deep within us, giving us strength to attain greater things.

John is quite explicit in his use of these words but if we take a quick overview of all the Letters – the marginal notes show where these words are concentrated, S or L etc. – it becomes clear that the power of divine love is attainable at *all* times to support our own pursuance of it in *all* our doings. The Letters as a whole become a wonderful tapestry of all the selected words, which shows in beautiful colours the whole fabric of redemption and salvation – as a modern aspect of our otherwise fairly fraught human existence.

Christ also uses the word 'sin' in addressing the woman taken in adultery but he does not say, 'do not commit adultery again,' but 'do not *sin* again' (Jn 8:11). That is a big challenge; but one he would not have made were it not attainable: an aim (commandment) to follow, not an examination to pass. He attunes her attention solely towards the future. There is no mention of the life problems that brought her to where she was, for we all have life problems. Knowing John's message now, we can see that what she has to learn to keep going on the right path is love. How did the rest of her life work out? What is she doing now? We can but wonder with creative imagination.

Rembrandt painted this scene with moving honesty. There is much darkness around her accusers while she herself is clothed in white, with the illumination falling upon her from above – a glimpse of the Spirit to come perhaps. Jesus is standing at the edge of this beam, a figure straight with true righteousness and so taller than all the others.

The story of the woman does continue however. He tells her accusers, 'You are from below; I am from above. You are of this world; I am not of this world. That is why I told you that you would die in your sins. For unless you believe that I AM I, you will die in your sins.' (Jn 8:23f).

The usual translation 'I am he' has been rendered as the original text, 'I am I', where Jesus reveals the cosmic or universal dimension of his 'I', his divine individuality. He has also just said 'I am the light of the world'. That is the point upon which we can pin our hopes, that this light is ever-existent and ready to illumine for us the right way forward. This will not be a *general* commandment to us but an opening up of an *individual* path – leading us to others.

The commandment to love is therefore not a prescription but a power, when felt aright. It is an example of how human life can now work along lines quite different from before.

There is much about sin in these Letters, but it is lightened and warmed through by the promise of divine love if we search for it – and give it out again. A glimpse at the state of the world may provide us with a hint that there is something important here.

Epilogue

The mysterious passage mentioned at the beginning of Chapter 2 (1Jn 5:6) is not easy to translate, due to different manuscripts having incomplete versions. Here a meaning is captured through the tone of the rest of John's Letters and his description of the crucifixion, where such emphasis is placed on there having been blood *and* water issue from the lance wound (Jn 19:34) after Jesus 'breathes his last'. The parallel between blood, water and breath with Jesus' life, soul and spirit and the members of the Holy Trinity, seems to make transparent sense.

The picture is widened by Steiner in an early lecture: 'A significant saying is to be found in the Bible [1Jn 5:7]. "For there are three that bear record in heaven: the Father, the Word and the Holy Spirit." And there are three that bear witness in earth, the spirit, the water and the blood.'*

The three elements of Jesus' bodily nature at the crucifixion are therefore images of the Trinity. Jesus' last breath was air, in Greek the same word as Spirit; then come the water and the blood from the wound. It is as though the

---

* Steiner, *Die okkulte Wahrheit alter Mythen und Sagen* (GA 92) lecture of Oct 21, 1904, p. 87.

three elements act as windows through which one may glimpse the members of the Trinity, rather as the bread and wine of the Eucharist are windows onto the risen nature of Christ Jesus. This comparison opens up the idea that blood, water and breath *are* the Trinity in a mystery sense. They reappear transmuted in the circle of the disciples on Easter evening, where the Risen One breathes upon them, saying receive 'holy breath' (usually translated 'Holy Spirit') and they share experiencing his resurrected body (Jn 20:22).

Steiner then goes on also to connect these three principles with the three higher, future members of the human being, Spirit Self, Life Spirit and Spirit Man, and he goes on to describe the intensity of feeling that the early Christians had for these images, touched upon so mysteriously and fleetingly in John's words. These higher human principles are nourished by the Holy Trinity through the sacrament renewed through the mystery of Christ and John, which the latter has made known.

We might also feel that this is a document that gradually embraces us with a kind of cosmic care and nurture; we come to realise that we 'abide' within it. It connects us both to the Holy Trinity, as an evolutionary dynamic rather than a transcendent deity, and to the personal development that arises out of this. We are embraced from without. But within? One cannot be embraced from within but can feel a renewed blood pulsing in the arteries, the blood of the vine filled with life and love, which can embrace the world.

I am sure that is what the Letters want to achieve and what we are able to achieve when reading with patience and imagination.

You may also be interested in...

Reflections on the Gospel of John

Johannes Lauten

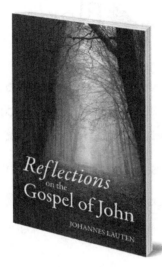

In this perceptive book, Christian Community priest Johannes Lauten reflects upon the many layers of meaning in John's Gospel. He explores some of the less well-known figures surrounding Christ, examines recurring words and phrases such as the 'Son of Man' and the seven 'I am' statements, and illuminates themes like knowledge, faith, the workings of grace and Christ's path to the Cross.

This thought-provoking book will be of interest to biblical scholars and those wishing to gain a deeper insight into the central meaning of Christianity.

florisbooks.co.uk

Floris
Books

For news on all our **latest books,**
and to receive **exclusive discounts,**
join our mailing list at:

florisbooks.co.uk/signup

Plus subscribers get a FREE book
with every online order!

We will never pass your details to anyone else.